Jurassic jungle!

You can see an Allosaurus (al-oh-saw-russ) here.
It is green with sharp teeth.

Can you spot the scuba-diving dinosaur?

Seek and Find
DINOSAURS

Illustrated by Emiliano Migliardo

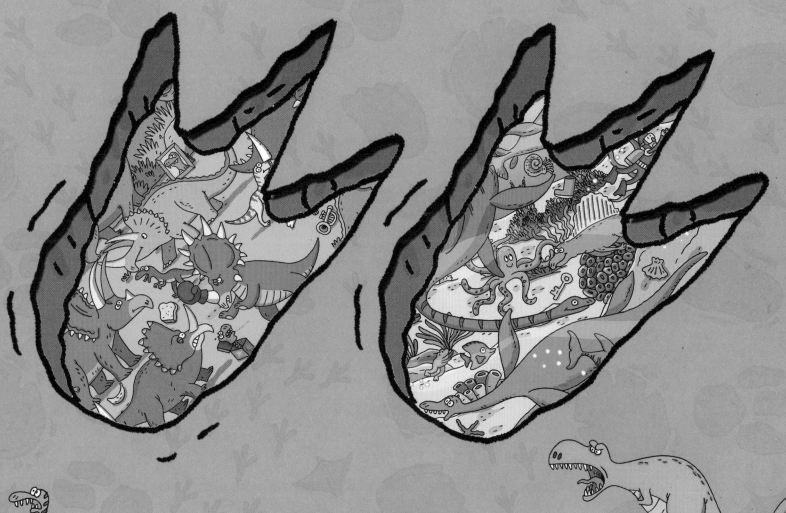

BLOOMSBURY
Activity Books

Welcome to the world of dinosaurs!

I wish I could fly!

Dinosaurs roamed the Earth millions and millions of years ago. We've learnt lots about them from their fossils. Some were big, some were small and some could even fly!

Can you find...

Wiggly, wriggly necks!

You can see the Argentinosaurus (ar-gent-eeno-sore-us) here. It was even longer than a blue whale and weighed as much as 15 elephants!

Can you see a dinosaur playing football?

Can you find...

Up, up and away!

Look at these flying dinosaurs! They are Pterosaurs (te-ra-sores).
They had wings like bats.

A superhero dinosaur is flying through the sky! Can you spot him?

Can you find...

Freezing forest!

Most dinosaurs liked warm weather but some visited snowy places.

Spot the two dinosaurs wearing the Santa hats!

Can you find...

How many horns?

Lots of dinosaurs had horns. You can see the Triceratops (tri-serra-tops) here. The[y] had two horns on their head, one on their nose and a big frill around their neck.

Can you spot the dinosaur with an ice-cream on its nose?

Can you find...

Ferocious feathers!

Some dinosaurs had feathers, just like birds do today. You can see the Archaeopteryx (ark-ee-opt-er-ix) here. This creature was about the same size as a crow.

🦶 Can you spot the dinosaurs having a pillow fight?

Can you find...

Diving dinosaurs!

The Plesiosaurus (pless-i-oh-sore-us) lived underwater. They had long snake-like necks and sharp teeth.

Can you spot the dinosaur wearing flippers?

Can you find...

The mighty T-rex

You can see the Tyrannosaurus (tie-ran-oh-sore-us) here. Some times called a T-rex, they were 13 metres long and could weigh up to 7 tonnes!

Can you see a dinosaur wearing glasses?

Can you find...

Dinosaur extinction

Millions of years ago dinosaurs became extinct. This happened when asteroids from space hit Earth.

Can you spot the dinosaur listening to music?

Can you find...

Digging for Dinosaurs!

Scientists have found out lots about dinosaurs from their bones.
This kind of research is called paleontology (pay-lee-on-tol-uh-jee).

Can you spot the pirate burying his treasure?

Can you find...

DINOSAUR FACTS

Allosaurus

🐾 The Allosaurus had a big mouth with lots of sharp teeth.

🐾 It used its sharp teeth and claws to catch and eat its dinner.

Archaeopteryx

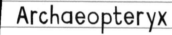

🐾 The Archaeopteryx had feathered wings, just like birds do today.

🐾 It's thought that it was one of the first creatures to fly.

Tyrannosaurus

🐾 This scary dinosaur had a mouth full of 60 sharp teeth.

🐾 It was longer than a bus and weighed as much as three hippos!

Argentinosaurus

🐾 These dinosaurs were probably the heaviest and longest creatures to ever walk the Earth! They grew to be longer than a blue whale and weighed as much as 15 elephants!

🐾 It took a baby Argentinosaurus a very long time to grow into a full sized adult!

Pterosaurs

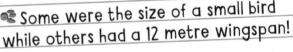

🐾 Pterosaurs were flying reptiles and soared through the sky using their powerful wings.

🐾 Some were the size of a small bird while others had a 12 metre wingspan!

Triceratops

🐾 It's thought that the Triceratops used their horns to protect them.

🐾 They were herbivores which means they only ate plants.